WIGGLE ROOM

TAKING A
BREAK FROM
BEING
PERFECT

Creative Editor: Laura LaTulipe

Tulip Editorial Services

Cover Photo: Angi Snyder

Back Cover Headshot: Heather Clark

Heather Clark Photography

Wiggle Room Press

JeniRoper.com

ISBN-13: 978-0-692-82467-2

For My Guys - Kyler and Collin

You are stronger than you'll ever know.

A HUGE thank you to all my Wiggle Roomies who believe in me and have waited so patiently for my book. It's because of you that there is SO much more to come! I *freakin'* love y'all!

Wiggle on, my friends!

FOREWORD
by Paul H. Jenkins, PhD

As you open this book, you might think that it is a collection of stories and musings of Jeni Roper. You probably picked this book up because you heard Jeni speak, or laughed your head off at a ridiculously pithy social media post, which she produces as regularly as most of us brush our teeth. Don't be deceived, consistent with one of the themes of this book, it is **not** about Jeni. *Wiggle Room* is about the lives that are enriched, blessed, and even saved as we get out of our own way and share our gifts with the world. Jeni just disguised it as an enormously entertaining and inspiring book featuring her wiggly self.

It is commonly said, "We don't see things as they are; we see things as we are." From subtle to severe, what we see is generally filtered through colored lenses—lenses that have been tainted, altered, colored by our experience. A friend once told me that everything we experience is as if it is projected on the inside of a box. Our mindset is that projection, and it is all we have. We can get out of our box, but the instructions for escape are printed on the outside of our box. That's why we need people like Jeni to read the instructions to us.

I can count on three things happening any time I interact with Jeni. I will laugh. I will cry. I will think differently. That happened again as I read this value-packed little book. Jeni embodies the concept that we are all perfectly designed to be imperfect. We're all just a little broken. Jeni gives us permission to be whatever we are in a more genuine and authentic way. To see her and listen to her speak helps us to see ourselves in a more truthful way.

So scooch on over and give yourself a little *Wiggle Room*, then share that gift with others—seriously, get another copy and give it to someone you love!

Paul H. Jenkins, PhD

Positivity Psychologist

www.DrPaulJenkins.com

TABLE OF CONTENTS

PART 1

On Your Mark,
Get Set,
WIGGLE!

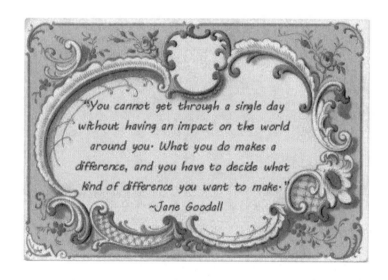

"You cannot get through a single day without having an impact on the world around you. What you do makes a difference, and you have to decide what kind of difference you want to make."
~Jane Goodall

A NOTE FROM JENI

I wiggle. Go ahead—be inspired. By all means, let the tears of awe fall. When I was a kid, I remember being in church and an elderly lady with a walker slowly made her way toward me from the back of the room. As she approached me with tears in her eyes, she hugged me tightly and said, "You inspire me so much! You are so very *special!*"

I'm special? She didn't even know my name! For all she knew, I could've just killed and buried my cat! To inspire someone just because I have a disability? Back to the loony bin, Grandma!

Turns out she wasn't crazy. I've had thousands of people come up to me with tears in their eyes, calling me the "S" word. Sigh. I couldn't wrap my head around this. If I was going to inspire someone, it had better be something that I *did*, dang it! It has taken years, and lots of pain and bitterness to realize that I *did* do something.

I showed up. And showing up led to ALL sorts of adventures.

Recently, I started sharing some tidbits of these adventures to a few people, and the response has been overwhelming. I had no idea my quirky little life could cause such a ruckus. I've been encouraged to write some of these adventures down, along with things I've learned from them. I've even been told that *not* telling my story meant that I was robbing others of blessings.

Wait…what?

My story is just a story. My story. My trials. My successes. My life lessons. Doesn't everyone have those?

Here's the thing; my "a-ha" moment, if you will. We, none of us, get to choose who we inspire. Just by walking (or wiggling) into a room, people look, watch, and yes, *feel.* Kind of scary, eh? But it can also be enlightening. *Everyone* has a story. Trials, successes, life lessons. I share mine in hopes that you, my audience, will see *your* story and feel the amazing importance of it. Not in *spite* of your wrong choices or imperfections, but *because* of them. Giving yourself permission to not only be imperfect, but to also let others be inspired by your unique but perfect imperfections. Weird, right?

My challenge to you...

As you read, I put it in your hands to choose what you want to do with it. Whether this is to be a book of entertainment, of strength, of inspiration, or just something to read when you can't sleep—that's up to you. I'm just my own storyteller, and I'm so excited to be able to share it, in all of its imperfect glory, with you!

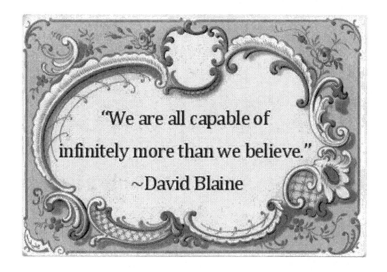

"We are all capable of infinitely more than we believe."
~David Blaine

TWENTY-EIGHT MINUTES

On April 30th, 2008, illusionist David Blaine appeared on a little program called *The Oprah Winfrey Show*, in an attempt to break the Guinness World Record for breath holding. He succeeded. Can you guess how long he held his breath? Four minutes? Seven minutes? Ten? Nah. The audience and the world watched in anticipation as David, in a small round tank held his breath for an amazing *17 minutes and 4 ½ seconds*. As unbelievably breathtaking a feat this was, I have one thing to say to Mr. Blaine:

You, sir, don't have anything on me.

My experience with breath holding was equally astounding, albeit highly unusual.

Moms and dads everywhere all have their own memories of how their little ones came into their lives. That one final push, one final moment that welcomes a living, breathing addition to their family. Wow. And while all of these 'miracle of birth' stories are all filled with their own perfect imperfections, thus is how *my* story began. Yes, there *was* a miracle that day in which my parents would tell over and over again, that miracle came just a little bit later than expected.

Mr. Blaine, I held MY breath for twenty-eight minutes. Neener.

When it became clear that my body was refusing to cooperate, nurses and techs tried CPR and everything else they could think of to get me breathing, but after ten to fifteen minutes, the doctor declared me stillborn. Two nurses (the first of *many* angels who came into my life) refused to give up. Everyone else had turned their attention to my mom, as they should, because she was hemorrhaging pretty badly.

Those two nurses not only saved, but they also *started* my life that day. After twenty-eight minutes of CPR, I took my first breath. I'm sure there was so much celebration. What an amazing miracle! I picture all the high fives, hugs, and tears that took place. A baby had been saved that day!

Over the next few days, however, for the doctors and nurses—and especially for my parents—the reality of this "miracle" started to set in.

Did you know that it can take an average brain just five minutes of being deprived of oxygen to start shutting down, causing irreversible damage? That fact undoubtedly hit everyone involved pretty hard. Later, my mom was told I would most likely live my life as a vegetable; never walking, talking, or having any hope of living a normal life. I often wonder if those nurses who started my life later regretted it, or were even disgraced by my doctor, knowing that I would have no valuable life or that I would be more of a burden to my parents than a blessing. If they ever did have these doubts, I hope that the know that were wrong, and I couldn't be more grateful.

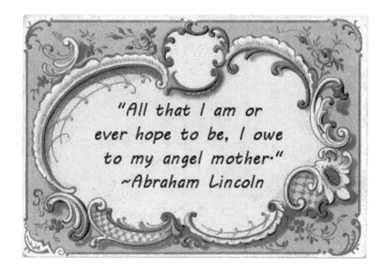

"All that I am or
ever hope to be, I owe
to my angel mother."
~Abraham Lincoln

GIVE ME WINGS

My mom often, frustrated by my asinine attempts to do "normal" things, asks, "Jeni, how on earth did you get so darn stubborn?" My response is always the same. In my most sarcastic, wise-arse voice I say,

"My *momma* raised me this way!" She then says,

"I raised you to be independent; not stubborn."

"One in the same, Mom." We've had to agree to disagree on this one.

My sweet mom chose to ignore the doctor's predictions that I would have no quality of life. She chose to listen to her heart instead. She knew that I wasn't saved in that hospital just to lie in bed my whole life. She saw something in my eyes that screamed, "Teach me to fly!" And that she did.

The doctor said that I'd never talk. I said my first word when I was a year old. It wasn't "Momma" or "Dadda" like a lot of first words are. It was "light." As Mom describes it, the word was clear as day, like I could have said it months ago, but was just being, well, stubborn.

The doctor said I'd never walk. I took my first steps when I was five years old. I actually have some faint memories of this. But it wasn't, "Oh look! Look! She's taking her first steps!" kind of thing that new parents exclaim as their babies just happens to decide that it's time. Nah. Getting this girl on her feet required work. And when I say work I mean it was my mom doing all the work. She'd put two chairs about two feet apart and every time I walked from one chair to the other, I would get my choice of a penny or a marshmallow. I would choose according to what my financial needs or tummy rumblings were at the time. My mom did this tirelessly for weeks, perhaps even months, until I was stable to walk on my own.

The doctor said I'd never have a chance at a normal life.

Yeah, right.

From an early age, I was taught the value of work. I had chores just as my siblings did. I was expected to keep my room clean (I can hear Mom laughing as she reads this). I cleaned up my own messes and was disciplined when I mouthed off. As I transitioned to school, my mom fought teachers year after year, to make sure I had all the adaptive tools I needed to succeed. At the same time, knowing that I was as intelligent as my classmates, she also fought for me to be treated as such.

I graduated high school at seventeen, and three months later, I headed to college two states away. Three years later, I flew across the country where I served eighteen months as a missionary for the LDS church. Two years after that, I married the man of my dreams, and eleven months after that, I achieved my lifelong dream—I became a mommy.

"Never have a chance at a normal life," my hiney. To that well-meaning doctor, I say what I told David Blaine:

"Neener."

And it's all because of my angel mom who listened to her heart and taught me to fly. I'll never be able to express my gratitude to her for not only giving me life, but giving me *a* life.

I love you forever and ever, Mommy.

"If you weren't you, then we'd all be a little less we." ~Piglet

A LIL' BIT BROKEN

So yes, the twenty-eight minutes my brain was deprived of oxygen left me with a disorder called cerebral palsy. Specifically, mild to moderate spastic-ataxic cerebral palsy. Quite the mouthful (I still have to Google it to make sure I get it right). I could get all technical here, but I prefer to explain it my way, because well, I've kind of earned it. Are ya ready? Here goes:

I wiggle. And when I say I wiggle, I mean *I WIGGLE, baby!* From the top of my head to the bottom of my toes.

For those of you who need a just a little bit of an explanation, let's jump into an analogy. Most of us have had a cold shower one or twice in our lives. Imagine trying to play the board game Operation while in that cold water. Think about how tough it'd be because your whole body was constricting. If you dared to even try to grab that funny bone or Adam's apple, you'd make your fist as tight as you could, pull your arms close to your torso, and clench those tweezers so tightly just to control the shivers your body instinctively would make because of the ice-cold water pouring down on you.

When trying to control *my* movements, for some reason it's the same principle (and I don't even need to have freezing water raining down on me). My limbs pull into my core for balance, and sometimes it takes a *lot* of concentration to try to relax them again. When I'm home alone, it's much easier. But everywhere else, there's no telling what my brain will expect my body to do. My legs automatically bend inward for more balance. My arms and hands are always ready for a fall. And somewhere in there is my speech. Sometimes my vocal cords are so tight I can barely form words. (I've been asked several times on the phone if I were drunk. I love having fun with that one!)

When it's winter and icy and all of us have to walk carefully anyway, *my* muscles tighten up so much that just to focus on what my legs need to do to keep my balance is a huge challenge. And it's not just ice. It's stairs or hiking, or even walking into my kids' messy room. People make the misconception that I get tired or hurt going up or down stairs. My legs are surprisingly strong. It's the rest of my body…every muscle tightening just to keep my balance. I make quite a spectacle just walking to my mailbox every day.

So yeah, long meetings exhaust me. I have to worry about shaking hands and what my right hand will decide to do THIS time. And that worry causes my muscles to tighten all over again! I worry about not having enough *wiggle room* and ending up accidentally palsy-punching the lady next to me. When I clap, will my hands open? I have no idea. When I'm in that situation where I have no control of what happens next, my muscles get tighter, and that's when the fun starts.

Let's take a minute to talk about my *good* hand. If you happen to hand me something, expect me to grab that sucker like my fingers and thumb are supercharged magnets that are attracted to each other. If you hand something to me, it better be indestructible. Styrofoam cups? CRUNCH? Ice cream cones? CRUNCH! Flowers? Heh— funny story—once my roommate's boyfriend came by with some beautiful fresh lilies for her. She wasn't home, so he asked if I could give them to her. Yes, of course. But as he hands me these beautiful, yet fragile flowers, CRUNCH! All of the flowers fell to the side, their stems snapped and were just hanging there, swaying from side to side. We both stood there staring at them for the longest ten seconds of our lives. The worst part? No witty Jeni comment, no, "Oh my gosh. I'm so sorry!" Nope. Yours truly backed up and slowly closed the door, while my roommate's poor suitor never took his eyes off his precious, broken gift. They broke up a few weeks later. I'm sure it had *nothing* to do with the lilies. That's what I tell myself, anyway.

I could go on and on, but as much as I *love* talking about myself, trying to explain my wiggly body (even the *Jeni* way) can be exhausting. Sometimes a simple explanation is the best explanation.

I was at my son's school wiggling down the hall when I noticed a little guy, not more than six years old, watching me. As I got near and smiled at him, he smiled back and said so very innocently, "Well, you're just a lil' bit broken, aren't ya?" I proudly said,

"Well, yes, yes I am!" The boy smiled his acceptance, waved at me, and skipped away.

Well said, kid. Well said. Out of the mouths of babes, eh?

WATCH THIS

I used to hate it when people stared at me. It just reminded me of my disability. Or weakness, as I once saw it. But now that I'm a bit older, I don't mind so much. Heck, even I find myself staring at people who are different. It's human nature to be curious and to watch. In fact, that's what I prefer to call it. Watching.

I've always loved watching kids (okay, so that sounded a bit creepy). I love to see how their minds work—what their hearts are saying even if they can't form the words in their mouths yet.

I was pregnant with my Kyler when I was asked to help in the nursery at my church on Sundays. This consisted of trying to tame a whole classroom of kids between the ages of two and four. There aren't many who are cut out for this two-hour calling (myself included). But you see, my church leaders were very smart. They could spot a nesting pregnant lady a mile away, and *BAM!* They found themselves a nursery leader.

It wasn't my turn to teach that week, so I hung out in the back with the other teachers, at the ready to calm, soothe, and sit with the wigglers (the *other* kind). In the back of the room there were stacks of chairs, which looked dangerously close to toppling over, so one teacher stood guard to make sure the kids stayed clear of them.

One little guy, however, was determined to get to those chairs. He kept leaving his own chair to try to climb up the dangerous mountain. Each time, my co-helper would patiently take his little hand and lead him back to his seat. He'd sit there ten seconds, then head back to the Tower of Terror. The fourth time this happened, the nursery helper sat down in the boy's seat, placed him on her lap, and held him tightly. He resisted, but the short lesson was now over, and it was playtime. Oddly enough, the little guy had no more interest in the chairs, and went over to play with a cute little girl in a yellow dress.

That's the way it was seen by everyone in the room. Everyone but me, that is. I was accidentally *watching*.

Here's how it really happened. Right after the teacher got the kids seated and somewhat calm, she started her lesson. Shortly after, a dad brought his little girl in. She wore a sweet yellow dress. As there weren't enough chairs, the dad, not wanting to disrupt the lesson, asked his daughter to sit quietly on the carpet by the door until the lesson was over. She gladly agreed and sat down, folding her little arms.

The little guy in the back saw this and not wanting the cute girl to have to sit on the ground, headed back to get her a chair, only to be interrupted and led back to his seat. He tried so hard to stay seated, but every time he glanced at the cutie on the floor, he couldn't stand it, and he'd try again to get her a chair to sit on. And every time, he was gently chastised and led back to where he belonged.

As I sat back and figured all this out, the thought that kept going through my head was, "I almost missed it." What looked like a four-year-old's curiosity mixed with a little orneriness was actually one of the sweetest acts of chivalry I'd ever seen. I wondered how many other amazing things I had missed because I wasn't watching. I made a promise to myself right then and there that I would *watch* my own children, and to not miss the amazing things that might be clouded by frustration.

When Kyler colored all over the couch with a permanent marker and I was ready to put him in time-out until he was thirty, I heard that promise to myself...*don't miss it.* Upon further investigation, I noticed that deeply embedded in the scribbles were the letters K-Y-L-E-R. Something we had been working with him for months without success. He was so proud of himself! What an amazing achievement this was for him!

And I almost missed it.

When Collin took his favorite—and most expensive toy to school—and came home without it, I was furious. As I called him in and started lecturing him using my mom voice, telling him how much money we spent on it, and how irresponsible it was to even take it to school, I heard it again, very quietly. *Don't miss it.* I took a deep breath, sat down, and asked Collin what happened to his toy.

With his head down and still feeling the shame that I had just forced upon him, he said, "Well, yesterday I was bragging to all my friends how cool it was and all the things it does. My friend looked so sad and told me how lucky I was. So I gave him mine." Just like that.

I wrapped my arms around him, and through my tears and lump in my throat, whispered, "Don't ever change, kid!"

And I almost missed it.

The guys and I were at McDonald's during the busy lunch hour. In front of us was a mom with her mentally handicapped teenaged daughter. She was loud! Whooping, jumping up and down, and yelling gibberish. Her mom kept whispering in her ear, undoubtedly trying to calm her down, but to no avail. The other customers were visibly uncomfortable and had their heads down, my kids included. Then I remembered.

Don't miss it. I whispered to them something that shocked myself. I told them that it was okay to watch her. We did. We heard out of her many noises the words, "Happy Meal!" And saw in her eyes pure joy and excitement. The three of us 'got it' at the same time. Ky said, almost too loudly, "Mom, she's sooo excited to get her Happy Meal!" All of a sudden, the entire mood of the checkout area changed. The cute teenager's excitement became infectious. Heads were raised, smiles were replaced with looks of happy excitement. This kid was getting a freakin' Happy Meal, dang it! And for a few minutes we all celebrated with her.

As she turned to leave, her daughter singing and jumping with her Happy Meal in tow, the sweet mom turned to me and gave me a hug and thanked me for understanding. I imagined her getting strange and uncomfortable glances everywhere they went, but for five minutes in a crowded McDonald's, she was just a happy teenager whose excitement lit up a crowd of strangers.

I'll be forever grateful that my boys and I didn't miss it.

I guess being a parent has taught me that staring, or watching, isn't as bad as I used to think. So many people have noticed weird things about me that I see as embarrassing weaknesses. The way I carry a soft drink so I don't crush it or spill it. The way I stab a piece of meat with a fork and take a bite like it were a corndog. The way I put undershirts on upside down and inside out…and how it magically rights itself. To my surprise, people have actually come up to me and told me how much they admire how I adapt to tasks that seem so minimal to them, but are challenging to me. It makes them appreciate what they have, and sometimes actually gives them life hacks to try for themselves. Go figure.

So go ahead. Watch me. I don't mind (most days). But not just me. As I keep saying, everyone has a story. *Don't miss it.*

PART II

Wiggle Giggles

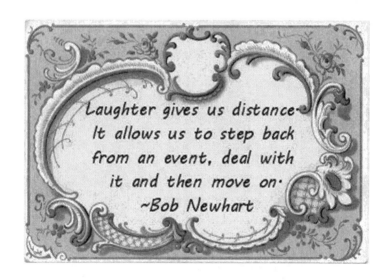

Laughter gives us distance. It allows us to step back from an event, deal with it and then move on.
~Bob Newhart

DON'T· DO· DRUGS!

Wiggling down the sidewalk one day, I noticed a group of teenage boys walking behind me. They seemed to be walking extra close, so I went on high alert and listened. I heard snickering, the sound of their footsteps in mocking tandem to mine, and a few "*durs*" and "*duhs*."

Wiggling around for as long as I have, I can tell you this is a common occurrence—in some form or another. There was a time in my life when this sort of teasing, and dare I say bullying, was *very* hurtful. As an adult, I know that behind every *potential* bully is just a kid trying to figure out his or her own self-worth. And when you think about it, when *any* of us, no matter how old we are, find ourselves in uncomfortable or awkward situations, we try our best to diffuse the awkwardness, even if it's at the expense of someone else's feelings.

Armed with this knowledge, as I heard the boys' mockings behind me, I decided not to be offended. On most days when this stuff happens, I ignore it, or politely make eye contact, smile, or wave. On this particular day, however, I was feeling a little…ornery.

With a smile I enjoyed a little too much, I stopped short, turned around, looked them right in their eyes, pointed my wiggly finger at them, and said very slowly, as I enunciated every word, "Don't. Do."—and then, pointing at myself—"Drugs!" I then turned around and wiggled away, leaving them speechless with their mouths wide open.

I don't know what took place with those boys after that day, but I'd like to believe a few things happened.

I don't think they've ever forgotten that experience.

I hoped they learned to think twice about teasing others who are different.

And you know what? I don't think that they *ever* did drugs!

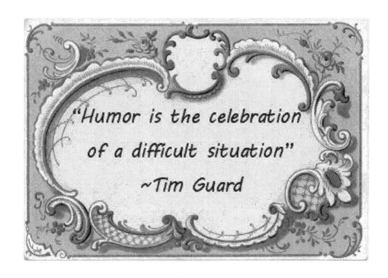

"Humor is the celebration
of a difficult situation"
~Tim Guard

THE FRIEND PROGRAM

When I first moved to Utah, I loved walking everywhere. It gave me the independence that I never had in my small, but widespread town in California.

One day my good friend and I decided to walk to McDonald's (back when they had the *good* fries). One of the things that defines a great friendship for me is someone who isn't even the least embarrassed to be with me, who ignores the looks and stares they get when they're with me. Even better, someone who is proud to be with a wiggler, and laughs with me about it.

Michael was one of those friends. We grew up together, and as a teenager we'd go to youth dances, and not only did he dance with me when all the other boys were terrified of me, but he'd also pull me out on the dance floor when no one else was dancing. In a place in my life that I literally hated myself and my life, Michael was one of my first friends who embraced every single wiggle I had, and loved me for them. He convinced me that he liked being with me and didn't just feel sorry for me. Guys, for a sixteen-year-old who thought of herself as a monster, this was huge. Though I wouldn't realize it until much later in my life, Michael taught me that I had value.

As we were about a block away from the Golden Arches, I noticed a fellow who seemed to be following us. I wasn't afraid, just a bit curious. We arrived at our destination, ordered, and headed to a table. Sitting down, I realized that yes, we had been followed because the same guy I saw a block away was approaching our table. I still wasn't afraid, but I had a fry in my hand, dipped in ketchup and ready to throw at him it if need be.

He turned to Michael, and the conversation went something like this,

"Hi there! I noticed you two walking here and thought I'd tell you that I think you're awesome, bro!"

"Um, thank you…?"

"Seriously, the world needs more people like you."

"Okaaay…"

Then, motioning ever so slightly toward me, "So are you with some kind of volunteer program?"

Michael was starting to understand.

"Um, this is Jeni—my *friend.*"

The stranger smiled at him and winked, as though to say,

"Riiiight. Your *'friend.'*"

Michael didn't break eye contact. He just slowly shook his head at the guy until he stuttered back, "Oh. Oooh. Okay, well then. Ahem…" and headed to the door without ordering anything (sad, because those fries were pretty dang good). Michael turned back toward me, shrugged his shoulders, and we continued our conversation like nothing ever happened.

I'm sure this guy had a big heart and the best intentions. But ignorance can sneak up on the best of us. That's why I love my Michael so much—he's never phased by situations like this. When I'm with him, he makes me feel normal. Friends like Michael remind me that I have amazing qualities that have nothing to do with my wiggles.

Yup. Everybody needs a friend like Michael.

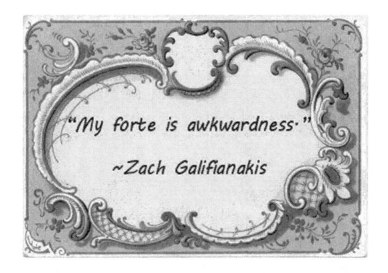

SQUEAK, SQUEAK

I always get so nervous when it comes to doc-tors. I don't know why. Maybe it's because I know they'll see my every little wiggle and twitch no matter how hard I try to hide it.

On this particular visit, the ole doc decided it was time for some lab work. Oh joy. I don't know what's more nerve-racking—the pain of getting blood sucked out of my arm, or the humiliation of urinating in a container comparable to the clear plastic cups that my sister had at her wedding re-ception.

No competition. The humiliation trophy goes to the stuff in the punch cup (or, as it turned out, the stuff that *wasn't* in the cup).

The seemingly simple task was very stressful for me. I always had horrifying thoughts about what *could* happen when called upon to make my little deposit, but I've always come out with little or no embarrassment. Until now.

Things were going okay. I had filled me little container and was well on my way to an embarrassment-free situation…when it happened.

I was carefully placing my precious cup onto the counter when—instead of sitting upright like cups are supposed to do—it…tipped. Now, when I say tipped, I don't mean it spilled a couple drops, I make a fast save, and say, "Oops, that was a close one!" Oh no. There was no quick save here. The cup, along with the contents thereof, went splashing onto the tile floor. Out of all the thoughts I could have been thinking at that very moment, the first one to enter my mind was, "How the heck am I going to get out of *this* one?"

Take just a second to put yourself in my shoes (which, by the way, were only a little wet). There I was, very exposed (I hadn't pulled up my pants yet), in a tiny, but extremely sanitary bathroom with very paper-thin walls. May I also point out that it was a slow day for the lab people, so they were waiting for me and counting the seconds.

I can't say that what I did next was what a proper young lady should have done, but it was all

I could think of. I started pulling paper towels out of the dispenser. One by one, I must have pulled out twenty or so and absorbed my mess. But because I had now made their clean little bathroom very unsanitary, my conscience got the best of me. Since I didn't feel like opening the door and yelling, "Hey, I just peed on your floor. You might want to bring in some bleach and a mop," I opted for another solution.

More paper towels.

This time they were soaked in water, with squirts of pink hand soap on them. I soaped up the floor, and then wiped it all up with more paper towels. I thought I might be in the clear. I mean, this whole process had taken a little over five minutes, which wasn't unusual. I looked at my cup, and miraculously, there was a tiny sample still in it, which would have to do. I scrubbed my hands three times then looked at the floor.

No evidence whatsoever of my mishap. I did it! No one will ever know. I actually had a hint of a smile when I opened the bathroom door. I had fought misfortune and won! I had conquered! But then I took my first step out of the bathroom.

Do you ever notice the sound your feet make as you're walking? I don't…unless it's an unusual sound. Well this noise, this horribly incriminating noise, was the worst sound that could have been heard at this very moment. It got louder as I walked toward the counter.

Squeak, squeak, squeak!

All the lab people turned and looked at me. It sounded as if I had just come in from the pouring rain.

I signed my papers and got out of there as fast as I could. I never looked back, because I just knew that if I did, I'd see the cleaning lady being told to go in there with a bottle of bleach and a mop!

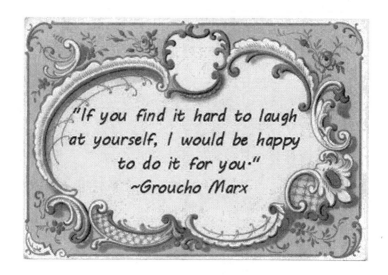

"If you find it hard to laugh at yourself, I would be happy to do it for you."
~Groucho Marx

ONE BUS PASS, PLEASE

I don't drive (legally—shhhh!), so I get the unfortunate privilege of relying on public transportation. When I first moved to Utah, one of my first priorities was to purchase a bus pass. I walked to the nearest ticket office and got in line. The sign read as follows, "Standard Monthly Bus Pass…$25.00." I dug deep into my pocket, pulled out the cash, and slapped it on the counter. "I'd like a bus pass, please." I smiled and slid over my twenty-five big ones.

The young guy at the counter looked at me kind of weird, nodded, handed me a bus pass, and then said, "That will be ten dollars!"

I was confused. "Ten dollars? Are you sure?" As pleased as I was, I needed an explanation.

My young friend pushed fifteen dollars toward me. "Yes, I'm sure. Have a good day." He cleared his throat and glanced behind me at the next person in line. Sadly for him, I wasn't done with him yet.

"Um, I don't mean to sound ungrateful, but could you explain to me why this sign says passes are twenty-five dollars, and you're only charging me ten dollars?" I was clearly frustrating the young man. He kept clearing his throat, and he even started stuttering a little.

Just about then I solved this great mystery. On the bottom of the sign, in fine print, read, "Persons with Disabilities…$10.00."

Although this information satisfied my curiosity, I sensed a wonderful teaching opportunity, and I took it (okay, okay, so *maybe* my ornery side took over). He still needed to answer my question.

"Ten dollars is the price of *your* bus pass."

"*My* bus pass?" I turned to the person behind me and smiled. "I must be pretty special, huh?" I was enjoying this a little too much.

"Look. This price is for *you*." He then quickly corrected himself. "I mean, it's for you, um, *people*."

Oh, my. This poor kid was getting himself in deeper and deeper. I decided to help him out, mainly because if he cleared his throat one more time, he might have injured himself internally.

"Oh!!" I tried to sound as surprised as I could. I also thought it important to raise my voice just a tad. "You mean I don't have to pay that much because I'm *disabled*!"

That poor kid! I don't know which emotion was more prevalent, the relief of me figuring out the mystery, or the embarrassment of me saying the "D" word so loudly. I leaned very close to him, and in a much lower voice said, "You know, that's not a dirty word. You should try saying it sometime." I winked at him, grabbed my fifteen dollars and my precious bus pass, and walked away. When I glanced back for one last look, his mouth was still open.

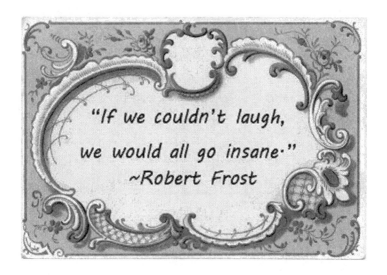

EXCUSE ME WHILE I FAINT

One particularly hot day of summer, as I waited for a bus, I wasn't exactly sure what side of the street I needed to be standing on., so I picked a side and watched the other very carefully. Sure enough, here came my bus—on the other side of the street. I grabbed my bag and started to run. Side note here: Disabled people (or at least *this* disabled person) look pretty dang funny when we try to run. You should watch, sometime.

Out of the very few times this wiggly chick has decided to run, this one will prove more regrettable than any of the others. As I started to cross the street, I forgot about the curb. You know that little thing on the edge of the sidewalk that anyone with half a brain would know to step *off* of? Pretty embarrassing…and painful. On the way down, the top of my foot kind of bent all the way backward.

Just in case you're wondering, the foot is not *supposed* to bend that way.

Lucky for me, this cute little gentleman was right there to help me up. Since I often rely on my one-track mind to get things accomplished, I decided to be a brave little camper and go with my original plan, which was to catch my bus. I crossed the street, not even realizing how much my foot hurt. I climbed up into the bus and sat down. Right away, I felt this funny, sort of woozy feeling come over me. Before I could figure out what was going on, everything went black. The next thing I remember was waking up lying across the seat wondering what the heck I was doing sleeping on the bus.

I could barely hear the bus driver asking, "Ma'am, are you okay?" I guess he was trying to find out if I really passed out or just fell asleep. At the same time, I realized I was *not* okay, which scared me. I darted up—big mistake—and announced I was about to throw up. The bus driver quickly grabbed his trash can and pushed it in my direction, but before I could take it, I was out again! This time I awoke to sirens—and about four paramedics touching, poking, and asking me tons of questions. They carried me to the ambulance, where I received the royal treatment.

I can imagine what the paramedics were thinking. *"Is she having a stroke? A seizure? Writhing in agony?* Poor guys. When I told them I had CP and that it was normal for me to wiggle like that, they collectively let out a huge sigh of relief. Then something *amazing* happened. They continued to take care of me as if I were a perfectly normal, intelligent patient! They took me to the hospital, where I was poked and prodded, then sent home.

This is one of those times that reminds me what it must be like for an outsider to try to look into the wonderful life of Jeni. I'm so very grateful for skilled medical technicians who aren't afraid of my wiggles. We need more people like that in this world.

"People will stare. Make it
worth their while."
~Harry Winston

BORED NO MORE

As a teenager, I was absolutely in love with my nieces and nephews. I always looked for those itty-bitty *aww* things to buy for them. I went to Walmart one day to look at baby shoes. There's just something about little pink booties that make them flat-out adorable. I glanced up to find a rather bored-looking middle-aged man (no doubt waiting while his wife tried on generic Nikes in size eight). This man seemed to find temporary relief by staring at me. After a few seconds, I smiled at him. This usually embarrasses the starer just enough to quickly get him interested in something else…like ceiling tiles or the stuff stuck underneath his fingernails.

This man, however, was an unashamed exception to the rule. In fact, he even found the nearest clothes rack, leaned his full body weight on it, and settled in to watch whatever I—and my odd little body—would do next. He was enjoying this a little too much.

I should mention I was only about sixteen years old at the time. Since I was a teenager, I despised being stared at.

I guess you could say I had an evil thought…and followed through with it. If he wasn't watching me so closely, he would have missed it. But this guy was all mine!

I picked up the smallest pair of pink booties I could find, held them up, gave the man full and complete eye contact, and slowly—but ever so affectionately—caressed my stomach.

I, with my sixteen-year-old imperfect self, convinced a perfect stranger—with one small gesture—that I was pregnant!

Poor guy! His mouth dropped open so wide he could have probably fit his wife's size eights in it. He gave me a *well-I-never* look, turned around, and walked away, grumbling to himself.

Shame on me.

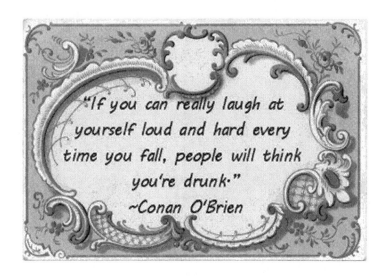

"If you can really laugh at yourself loud and hard every time you fall, people will think you're drunk."
~Conan O'Brien

BLACK ICE AND AN OIL CHANGE

I lived in Idaho for three years while I attended college. I loved every part of the blessed place, except for one thing: the winters. Before I moved there, I didn't know the meaning of the word cold. And what's worse than the cold air? One word: ICE! I would see my able-bodied friends slip on the stuff daily, so you can imagine the kind of problems I had. You can also imagine the fun I had laughing at my unfortunate encounters with this odd element of nature.

For one of my classes, I had to visit an elementary school classroom. So about ten of us piled in a big van and went together. When the day was over, we were all tired, hungry, and ready to go home. My roommate and I were the last ones to make our way to the van, and since there was about two inches of ice covering the entire parking lot, we took our time.

We were doing okay, but the van was about ten feet away, and my tummy was growling. I don't know if I was overconfident, too anxious, or too hungry, but something happened. My left foot touched a patch of unstable ice (or maybe the ice touched my unstable left foot), and everything went blurry. Three seconds later, when I opened my eyes, I found I was lying flat on my back. If that was all to the story, it wouldn't be worth writing, because it was common to find myself on the ground while attempting to walk on ice. But that's *not* all.

I looked up toward the sky, but the sky had disappeared. I found what was blocking my view was nothing other than the underside of some sort of a vehicle!

That's right, folks!

I had fallen and slid right under a parked car!

I, of course, found the humor right away and started to laugh hysterically. My roommate—who was also busting up—grabbed me by the hand and started to pull me.

When you think of the ice, the laughing, and the lack of motor skills on my part—we didn't get very far. I should mention again that there were eight people in a van ten feet away that I'm sure found this very amusing.

It took about ten minutes for me to get out from under the car, get my feet under me again, and make my way back to the van. Needless to say, everyone laughed all the way home!

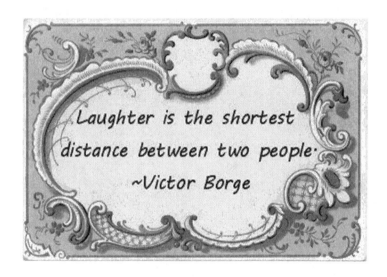

Laughter is the shortest distance between two people.
~Victor Borge

INVISIBLE WIGGLES

I attended a writing event for the greatest minds in my area. It was my first time in this group, so I played it safe and listened and observed. Very unusual group, but that's another fifty-thousand-word book.

Also in attendance was an assertive, yet very friendly gal named Brooke. It was her first time as well, and she was eager to make friends. She went around the room and asked for names. There were four of us seated at one end of the table, almost in a perfect row. "Your name is…? And yours…?" I was getting ready to offer up mine when—yup. She *skipped right over me* and proceeded to the person to my right. "And what was your name…?" I looked back and forth, wondering if she couldn't see me. Nope. Line of vision was clear. So I raised my hand high in the air and said, "Um…hi! I'm Jeni!" She looked at me with a very awkward smile.

"*Ahem*…oh…um yeah. Okay…nice to meet you."
I just grinned at her until she became intensely interested in the button on her blouse.

Even with all of my experience with people who are very uncomfortable when they're around me, I'm still shocked (but not surprised) every time they try to hide it. There I was, the most wiggly person in the room, and Brooke—bless her heart—chose to deal with it by pretending I wasn't.

I always think it's my job to make others feel comfortable around me and my wonderful wiggles; and maybe it is. But maybe…*I* need to give *others* the wiggle room that they need to feel what they're going to feel.

Huh. Maybe I'll learn something from this book after all.

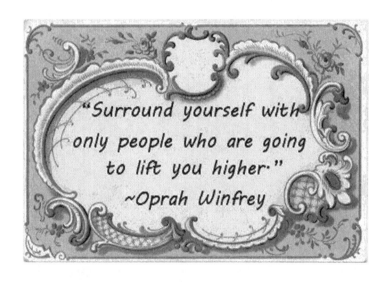

EIGHTEENTH-STORY CARRY-OUT

A tiny bit of trivia. The Zions Bank Building, deep in the heart of Salt Lake City, is exactly eighteen stories high.

It was my first meeting at the National Speaker's Association—the NSA—(the ones who speak, *not* the ones who listen) and I was nervous. I was told the best of the best speakers would be there, and because I wanted—no, needed—to be a speaker, I needed to rub shoulders with these giants (literally, because former Jazz player Mark-"Seven-Foot-Four" Eaton was there).

The meeting started at three in the afternoon, but I was up at six because I was so excited and nervous. When my colleagues arrived to pick me up, I had changed my outfit about four times and put deodorant on six times. The forty-five-minute ride felt like five hours.

We reached the Zions Bank Building, made the very quick elevator ride to the eighteenth floor, and entered the beautiful Founders Room. We were a teensy bit late, so we tried to sneak in and find our seats in the back.

Those who know me know I don't "sneak" anywhere. All eyes—or so it seemed—were on this wiggly being who just walked through the door. By the time we found our seats, I realized I hadn't breathed in a while (something I've done before). My brain decided it needed oxygen, so I spent several minutes wheezing and gasping for air as if I had *walked* up those eighteen flights of stairs.

Just as my breathing returned to normal, I could see the NSA chapter president at the front of the room speaking actual words I was starting to understand. I relaxed a bit. This wasn't so intimidating.

Then I heard it. The most dreaded sound since kindergarten. The pulse-piercing sound of a fire alarm. My friends tell me all the color drained from my face, and my eyes glazed over like a Krispy Kreme doughnut. Eighteen flights of stairs.

People started migrating toward the stairs. Not the elevator—the stairs. Eighteen flights. Women were taking off their high heels for the trek. As I walked with the herd, as slowly as I could, it was all I could do not to duck into the next room, hide under a table, and hope a nice fireman would save me.

As I wiggled down the first few steps, it was quite evident to me—and everyone else around me—that yes, even though I *could* do this, the building would be burned to the ground and the firemen would be home having dinner with their families before I made it out.

So my buddy Darren had a brilliant idea. He grabbed the closest guy and suggested they use the fireman's grip to carry me down eighteen flights of stairs. Basically, they linked their arms together to form a seat, I sat on said seat, and got carried down. Eighteen flights of stairs. My hiney on their arms. For eighteen flights of stairs.

Everyone was laughing and teasing and having a jolly ol' time. My other buddy got his camera and tried recording it. I could tell my brave heroes were getting tired and were starting to hurt, but I had to admit, I had other things to worry about.

Having cerebral palsy means I sometimes don't have control of my body. Most people *don't* realize this entails my outer body…and my inner bodily functions. (I'll let that sink in a little bit…) Yup. For eighteen flights, the only thing I was thinking and praying was, "Please, please don't fart or pee on these two gentlemen."

Thankfully, we made it to the lobby and my fearless champions set me down. Exactly in time to hear someone say, "Yup, it was a drill, folks. You can all go back in." I *really* wanted to lunge at the dude and go for the jugular, but my bum was numb.

As we crammed ourselves into the blessed, glorious elevators, I had to giggle at the situations that I'm presented with. And I'm grateful.

Grateful for the chance to meet amazing people. Grateful for surprises. Grateful for an invention called the fireman's grip. Grateful for my buddy who suggested it. Grateful for the stranger who didn't hesitate to help. Grateful there wasn't an actual fire. But most of all, I'm grateful that I was in control of my bodily functions—for all eighteen flights.

PART III

Wiggle Wisdom

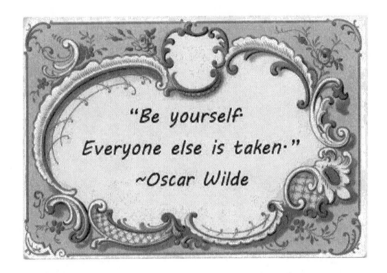

WISE WORDS, BUT...

Busy waiting rooms are a big part of my life. I don't mind. People watching is ironically, one of my favorite pastimes. You know how sometimes these waiting rooms have big-screen televisions that play short snippets of advice that tell us how to live healthier? Maybe it's just me, but for some reason, listening to some doctor in Australia telling me how bad doughnuts are for me never seems to make my waiting experience any more pleasant. I'd rather stick to people watching.

As I was waiting for an appointment one day, I was absentmindedly staring at the screen. My eyes became immediately focused when I saw a college student being interviewed. He was in a wheelchair, and obviously had cerebral palsy. It was a very short clip and difficult to hear over the hustle and bustle around me, but the gist of the story was focused on this kid being an advocate for people with disabilities, specifically those going to college. He had rallied and petitioned colleges throughout the nation to have accommodations for students in wheelchairs in every single building. His interviewer was the great Oprah Winfrey who praised his efforts and was amazed at how much he had accomplished. I watched with goosebumps and a teeny bit of jealousy because he got to meet the amazing Queen O. What an inspiration this guy was to me, Oprah, and thousands of others. The world needs more people like this.

As the interview came to an end, Oprah asked one last question; one that I have been asked many times myself, "How are you able to maintain such a positive attitude while having a disability?" His answer was unforgettable.

"Well Oprah, I just take my disability and all the problems that come with it and set it aside. What's left, *that's* the real me, and I act accordingly."

I could just leave the story right there, and it would be inspiring as it was for Oprah and thousands watching. What an amazing guy.

Do you ever hear something really inspirational, but realize that even if it blows your mind, that a tidbit of that message isn't really applicable in your life? The more I thought about this kid's message, the more I realized it was very different than what I've learned, and the message that I share.

For years, I tried just that. Putting my disability over to the side, and trying to be the girl underneath. I tried to prove to people that I was "normal" beneath my flawed, awkward, and very noticeable body. It didn't work. Trying to pretend (and expect others to also pretend) that I wasn't any different than anyone else was like wearing a clown suit to church and expecting people to act natural. It just wasn't happening.

My wiggles don't define me; however, they are a part of who I am. I'm a mom, an athlete, an author, a speaker, a Collin Raye fan, a mentor, *and* I wiggle. I can't very well hide the fact that I'm a mom (nor would I want to). Why then, did I even try to pretend that my wiggles aren't a part of me? They've played a huge part in the reason I choose to live my life the way I do. It now makes no sense to me to try to put my disability aside and still try to be me.

It was only when I realized this that I started to love myself. I could look at myself in the mirror and see my flaws, *and* I could see a very *real* person with my own set of gifts. A person simply can't have one without the other. We're not designed that way. *We are all divinely designed for perfect imperfection.* And it's through this perfect imperfection that we find happiness in this crazy life.

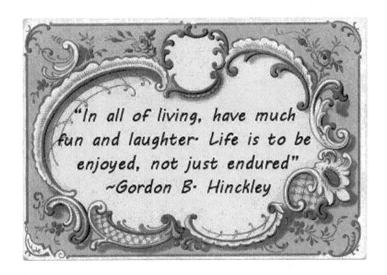

"In all of living, have much fun and laughter· Life is to be enjoyed, not just endured" ~Gordon B· Hinckley

SURVIVING BOB

Can someone please tell me why roaches were put on this earth? Seriously. I've never heard anyone say, "Aww, look at that cute little roach!" Or, "The interesting thing about roaches is…" They're ugly and creepy and can survive the apocalypse. We get it.

Oh yeah. And they come in different sizes. There's a huge size difference between the roaches in California and say, northern Florida. For example, in Crestview, Florida, to squish a roach it takes a running start, a long jump, and a landing with both feet. Then there's Texas. The roaches there live up to the "everything is bigger" cliché. And then some.

When I was an Especially for Youth counselor, I spent a week at the beautiful campus of Austin College in Sherman, Texas. As a counselor, I was able to hang out with amazing teenagers twenty-four seven. I was the fearless leader of anywhere between twelve and eighteen girls each week. The days were jammed packed with classes, activities, dances, and as my girls would say, BOYS! You would think that as busy as we were during the day, my little flock of girls would collapse in their beds and sleep soundly through the night. Those who have ever been around teenagers are reading this and shaking their heads with a knowing grin that says, "Nice thought, but nope!" Not only are they awake, but awake and giggly. And hungry. Always with the hunger.

This night was no different. As we got back to the dorms, I told my little giggly group to gather into one of their rooms as I grabbed my materials for our short nightly devotional. Five minutes later, I heard bloodcurdling screams coming from that very room. As I wiggle-ran down the hallway, doomsday thoughts were flying through my head. *Fire? Fatal injury? Intruder?* When I got to the room, all fourteen girls were huddled together. Eight on one bed, six on the other. Some were standing on the bed doing a horrified dance, and they were all screaming.

Quickly assessing the situation, I saw the cause of the panic. It was in fact an intruder. Looking down, I saw a roach the size of a small puppy skitter across the room and under the dresser. I added to the collective screams and hopped on the nearest bed. Like a mob rioting, things escalated quickly. Every time the thing ran across the room, more terrifying screams followed and a panicked conversation began.

"Get him!"

"Stomp on him!"

"Get a book and squash him!"

"NO! Not the Scriptures!!!"

"Aww, don't KILL him!"

"Go, Bob, GO!"

We all paused and faced one of my shyer girls, who shrugged and said, "What? He looks like a Bob, and he's kind of cute."

Another pause, and then…

"KILL him!"

"Can I switch rooms?"

"Oooh! I have a lighter…"

"Yeah! Torch him! Torch Bob!"

"NO LIGHTERS!" (that was me)

"Let's put a collar on him!"

79

SMACK! SQUISH! SILENCE.

One of my girls dropped a gigantic pizza box on Bob, and we all heard his fate. There were cheers, high fives, and hugs. We had faced our intruder, and we had conquered.

When things settled down a bit, my shy one spoke up, "Poor Bob. He fought so hard."

"She's right. He was a tough little guy."

"He WAS someone's offspring."

"He never gave up."

"We should have a moment of silence for good ole Bob."

At this point I knew that the warm and fuzzy feeling of a nightly devotional was never going to happen. So I decided to embrace the silliness. We all gathered around the oversized pizza box and bowed our heads. Ten seconds in, a scream. Then another. Then all fourteen girls. Again. The pizza box was moving! What fresh hell was this? Then, from under the box, Bob emerged. Dragging himself slowly with his one good leg. Barely, but still alive, he was determined to not go softly into the night.

With one swift motion, one of my girls slid the box back over Bob while three other girls jumped on top of the box and stomped like a three-year-old toddler throwing a fit. I was then elected, while the girls took cover on the beds again, to look under the box to make sure Bob was indeed deceased. Yes, not only had Bob crossed over to the other side, but he was permanently affixed to the bottom of the box. I grabbed the deadly weapon, ran down the hall, tossed it in the garbage bin, and slammed the lid tight—just in case.

And that was the end of Bob the roach. Now we know roaches can not only survive a nuclear bomb, but also a room full of teenage girls (well, almost). Somebody call Guinness.

How does Bob fit into my Wiggle Room story? One word—survival. Bob, along with his friends were engineered to, for whatever reason, survive. And they are very, very good at it.

Survival—one of the most powerful instincts that drives us. It's the reason we eat, sleep, breathe. Without this innate instinct to survive—to keep existing, human kind would have died out pretty quickly. But unlike our buddy Bob, we have so many other instincts. We weren't put on this earth to *just* survive. The second edition of *the Oxford English Dictionary* estimates that there are twenty-five thousand verbs in the English language. THAT's why we were sent here—to DO.

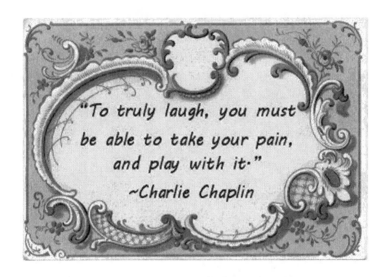

"To truly laugh, you must
be able to take your pain,
and play with it."
~Charlie Chaplin

THE TOUGH PART

The more I tell my story, the more I'm aware of the repetitive questions asked of me. The ones I'm asked almost daily all have the same tone to them.

"When did you stop being so bitter about your disability?"

"At what point in your life did you realize all that you've overcome?"

"How do you stay positive all the time?"

It's very interesting how all of these questions have to do with time. And dare I say a *specific point* in time.

My answers:

"I still get bitter."

"I still, and always will need to overcome."

And for heaven's sake, "I'm not even *close* to being positive all the time!"

So there ya go. The truth finally comes out.

While I'm kind of okay talking and laughing about my physical imperfections, I rarely talk about my inner imperfections. I wonder why that is sometimes.

While it's easy for people to be inspired by those who are fighting like hell to overcome the things that life throws at them, we tend to be less inspired by those fighting to overcome messes which have come about as a result of personal choices.

Guys, **depression is real**. Twenty years ago, the world was just learning this. Before that, it was believed that being sad or bitter or angry was a daily choice we made every morning when we rolled out of bed. I lived half my life believing this, and still struggle every single day.

Before you throw this book out the window and call me a fake, let me clarify. Happiness *is* a choice. And sometimes that choice involves being self-aware enough to know that we need *help* to achieve happiness. And for some, (dare I say most) the choice to be happy takes a *lot* of hard work.

Kind of makes you think differently about that coworker who is *always* a ray of sunshine, eh?

So, overcoming stuff? Being okay with my imperfections? Being positive? Nah. I've spent half my life being sad, angry, and bitter. But here's the kicker—this is *not* a chronological, "half my life." It is an up and down battle that I struggle with every single day.

I was twenty-three years old, serving a mission for my church in northern Florida, I was so very *angry*. And I had no earthly idea why. I woke up angry, got dressed angry, ate angry, and even brushed my teeth angry. When my fellow missionaries asked me why I was so angry, I'd just get angrier. And when I was all angered out, I felt guilty for being angry. The guilt turned into sadness, the sadness turned into depression, the depression turned into self-loathing, and the self-loathing turned into, yup you guessed it. Anger.

It wasn't until one of my leaders suggested I read a book called *Listening to Prozac* by Peter D. Kramer. Prozac was the buzz word of the year, and at a glance, I (along with the rest of the world) shrugged it off as a Band-Aid for sad people. Some still believe this, and that's okay. I'm certainly not advocating pill-popping.

For me, this book was life altering because it showed me that I wasn't alone. Other people out there were going through this stuff. There was actually a *name* for it—depression. Not the "my boyfriend broke up with me so let me be sad for a few weeks" depression. We're all meant to feel *that* kind of sadness. This kind of depression, the depression *I* felt, is the "fighting like hell every *single* day to survive—trudging through what felt like a mixture of mud and tar just to put a smile on my face and hope it'll be real someday" kind of depression.

I was absolutely shocked to find out that a huge part of clinical depression is anger. Weird, eh? We don't usually view a rude, annoyed, impatient person behind us in line at the grocery store with sympathy. We don't think she's depressed. We think she's just having a bad day, or we maybe even label them with adjectives that I'll not write in this very family-friendly book. The reality just might be that this person sat on her couch for three days to muster up the courage and energy to shower, dress, and drive to the store. Again, this kind of changes the way we look at people, huh? Like I said, life changing.

Any good driver carries a toolbox in their trunk, just in case something goes wrong. These tools are carefully chosen with one solitary purpose—to get their vehicle back on the road so they can reach their destination safely.

Part of opening my eyes to this newly defined disorder was realizing that there are tools out there to help me manage my depression. Just as no one is expected to change a tire without a jack, a person with depression shouldn't be expected to manage, or even overcome it without some tools to help them get back on the road of life again.

My Toolbox

Living with depression has required me to pick up lots of tools along the way. My own toolbox of survival, if you will. And having that toolbox has been a lifesaver, but *only* when I choose to pick up those tools and get to work. And yes. It *is* work. Every. Single. Day.

Some of my tools include medication, counseling, music, going for a walk, watching a movie that I've seen a hundred times but still makes me laugh, talking to a four-year-old (seriously, how can someone *ever* be sad while talking to a four-year-old?), exercising—the list goes on and on. But there are three tools that I consider absolutely essential, and I keep them in a special place in my box.

The most important tool in my toolbox is prayer. I have a very sacred relationship with God, and without Him, I wouldn't be where I am today. I need to tread very lightly here, but sometimes when I mention to my church leaders that I have depression, I am *always* lovingly encouraged to pray. Prayer works miracles—this I know. But somewhere in this great council, things get misinterpreted. There are times in my life where I am just trying to survive the next hour, praying my guts out, determined to not get up off my knees until I feel happy. Sometimes I wake up, *still* on my knees as my alarm clock goes off. I feel like I had failed. Why wouldn't God take away my pain? I must not have enough faith.

Guys, this is one of the biggest lies ever told—that faith is all that is needed to overcome anything. Nope. Just as a jack is probably the most important tool to change that flat tire, it's useless without a lug wrench. (Yes, I Googled that. Leave it to a wiggly non-driver to use a driving metaphor.)

The second essential tool in my toolbox is gratitude. This may be one of life's greatest mysteries. I honestly don't know how it works, but being grateful for stuff, actually *makes* good stuff happen. I've tested it over and over, and am always amazed at how much my spirits are lifted when I am grateful. Even for the teeniest of things. My friends on social media know that every night I post a "tonight I'm grateful for…" post. Sometimes they're insightful, but more often than not, they're light and just plain silly. But they *are* real things that I'm grateful for. When I say I'm grateful for socks, I really *am* grateful for socks. Or finding a hidden fun-sized Milky Way bar in the bottom of a drawer—that's pure gold! And acknowledging even the smallest of blessings lifts my spirits so very much.

The third essential tool in my toolbox is service (this is also one of the toughest tool to pick up). When I'm down and depressed, it's like I have blinders on. I can't seem to find a way out of the darkness. I was recently in this very condition, when a friend texted me that she missed me. It made me feel good, but the miracle happened after I asked *her* how *she* was doing. As it turned out, she was really struggling. My heart went out to her as I listened and was able to comfort her…however meager it was. Guys, this lifted me up so much! It's amazing what happens when we put our sadness aside to uplift someone else. As I said, it's not even close to being easy, but using this tool of service has *never* failed to shine light into my darkest times.

So back to those original questions. How do I stay positive? How do I overcome? I don't. But I don't try to do it alone anymore, and that brings hope, and ultimately joy beyond I ever thought possible.

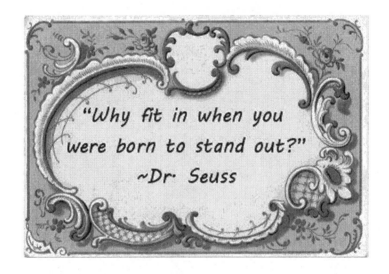

FRECKLES IN AN ELEVATOR

Years ago I worked for a mortgage company, one of my favorite jobs ever. I got to take on the big scary banks, help people modify their home loans, and save them thousands of dollars. And I kicked butt! I was able to save a few homes literally the *day* of foreclosure. Such a gratifying experience.

After working there for a couple of weeks, my boss pulled me into his office to chat. He told me about his two-year-old son who had cerebral palsy. He wasn't as fortunate as me. His son had to deal with heart problems and was in and out of the hospital many times that year. My heart was breaking as he told me about his tiny son's struggles. But then he smiled and told me of his son's amazing spirit, the wisdom in his eyes, and his spunky attitude. I could feel the fatherly pride in his eyes.

He shared that his biggest frustration was when they go out as a family and dealing with the "gawkers." I rolled my eyes and was about to tell him just how much I understood, and we could swap some stories and be annoyed together. But as he continued, I realized this *wasn't* where the conversation was heading.

Dave paused for a minute and his face changed to sadness. Emotional now, he said, "I just want to wave at them. To say, 'Come on over! Let me introduce you to my amazing son!' Then they would feel his spirit and not feel sorry for him, but feel blessed to get to know him for a bit."

What surprised me, and will stick with me forever, was that his feelings weren't as a protective parent trying to shelter his son from these rude people. His attitude was one of compassion for the people who were staring.

"If they only knew."

Not long ago, I found myself in a crowded elevator. Smack dab in the middle of this elevator was a red-haired, freckle-faced little guy who looked to be seven or eight years old. His limbs were twisted and contorted and sticking out beyond his wheelchair. In my two-second assessment of the situation, time slowed down and I remembered.

I remembered the courteous glances of those who had no idea how to react. I remember the look on my mom's face—one of pride and protection as she scanned the crowd. I remember learning to smile, even halfheartedly at these people, because they needed me to be okay with what was happening with my body. I remember wishing I could just *be*.

I knew what I needed to do. I looked the kid right in the eye, and exclaimed, "Holy cow, kid! Those are a *lot* of freckles! Wassup with that?" (I meant it, too. He was covered with them.) A huge *real* smile took up his whole face, and he laughed a *real* laugh. The kid's laughter was infectious, and the entire elevator seemed to light up.

The ride was quick—nothing else was said. But in that thirty seconds I was flooded with memories of when I was young, trying to make sense of the wiggly body that I'd been given. That old lady with tears in her eyes, telling me how special I was, the uncountable table pep-talks my sweet mom gave me about overcoming my challenges, the advice from church leaders about beauty being on the *inside*. Pshh. Yeah right.

I kept this anger and bitterness for years, and it still pops up every now and then. I still struggle with that word—"special." In my home, it's lovingly called the *other* "S" word. I so wanted, and still want, for people to *see* me.

See *me*. See that I love kids. See that my two true loves were Kirk Cameron and Michael J. Fox. See that I have a ridiculous sense of humor and that I mouthed off to my parents. See that my favorite season is summer. See that I wanted to be a mommy and a writer when I grew up, in that order.

We all want—and dare I say need—to be *seen*. The saying "she's the whole package" is the ultimate compliment. We want people to take the time to unwrap the package, regardless of our sloppy wrapping.

So yes, that day in that small crowded elevator, I hope I was able to give that little freckle-faced kid a little *wiggle room*, and acknowledge that for thirty seconds, I saw him not just as a poor kid in a wheelchair, but as a regular kid who probably had an attitude as fiery as his red hair, and probably gave his mom some serious grief.

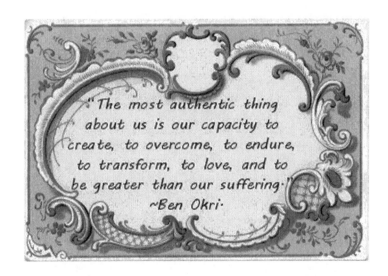

"The most authentic thing about us is our capacity to create, to overcome, to endure, to transform, to love, and to be greater than our suffering."
~Ben Okri·

DOING IT ALONE

During a meeting at church, a very well-prepared teacher had an amazing object lesson planned to show how our sins weigh us down and keep us from living a happy and fulfilling life. She pulled out a backpack and instructed an unwitting volunteer to put it on and fasten it securely. We watched with *ooohs* and *aaahs* as the teacher proceeded to put rocks into the backpack (each rock representing a sin). When our volunteer looked like she was going to topple over, our teacher zipped up the backpack and handed her a big bowl. Yup, more rocks. With the bowl filled to the brim and her back weighed down, she was instructed to go to the back of the room, open the door, go out, and then come back through the door on the other side of the room—with no help from any of us.

I'll be honest. I thought this was a little over-kill to make a point. But I *watched*. As she circled around to come in through the second door, she was really struggling to open it. I was sitting by that door and felt her struggle. After a few moments, my friend Beth—who was sitting by me—got up and said, almost under her breath, "No one should have to do this alone." She opened the door for our volunteer then sat down like it was nothing. The teacher jokingly chastised her for cheating. She relieved our brave volunteer and continued talking about the dangers of sin.

For me, however, the lesson could have ended right there. And the rest of the audience *missed it*.

My mom raised a very stubborn girl. I remind her every time she worries about me biting off more than I can chew. Independence was—and is—very important to me. Countless people have told me how much they *admire* me for my inde-pendence. It *inspires* them (there's that word again). Of all the labels I had, I was proud to be labeled as independent. If I fell, I got up—by myself. I was *independent*.

If I needed to be somewhere, I took city transportation, even though the cost was outra-geous to merely ride across town. I was *independent*.

I spilled more drinks, bowls of soup, and catsup bottles than a toddler. But that didn't matter—I was *independent.*

I was well into adulthood before I realized being independent was exhausting! At least what I believed independence was. I always got the job done, but the cost always paid its toll. After a while, exhaustion became depression. I'd find myself *almost* admitting I needed help. That my body wasn't as able-bodied as I needed it to be, and it was okay to accept help.

But then the trickster part of my brain would scream, "No! Your independence is why people like you! It *inspires* them! Without your independence, you'll just be one of those whiney cripples who take advantage of everyone!"

The trickster would always win, and to be honest, it still does sometimes. And this way of thinking almost always led to failure. So many activities were missed because I didn't want to pick up the phone and ask for a ride. So many cute clothes and shoes left on the rack in the store because they had tiny buttons or zippers—and I didn't want to ask for help getting dressed. So many times I turned down steak on a menu because I didn't want to ask for help cutting my meat.

This take I had on *independence* led to some pretty severe depression. Those who have experienced depression know that it can be a slippery slope. My depression led to anger. *Lots* of anger, especially in my teens and early twenties. I was angry at God for giving me an imperfect body, angry at other people my age for being "perfect," angry at my mom for having high expectations of me. I was even angry at the two nurses who kept performing CPR on me when I was born.

It took me years to figure out that no one on this earth is *independent. Duh.* None of us would be here without the help of other people. Such a simple truth, but that trickster part of my brain was keeping me from seeing it.

That Sunday when Beth opened the door for the rock-bearing volunteer and said very quietly, "No one should have to do this alone," stirred in me a much deeper lesson to be learned. For a moment, those rocks represented imperfections, challenges, frustrations, depression, and anger. I pictured myself carrying all those rocks, trying to ignore them as I proclaimed, "I GOT THIS!" to any who tried to open the door.

I'm constantly learning that I don't *got this*. I need help. Not just because I have a disability, but because I'm human. *Duh.*

Nobody should have to do this *life* alone.

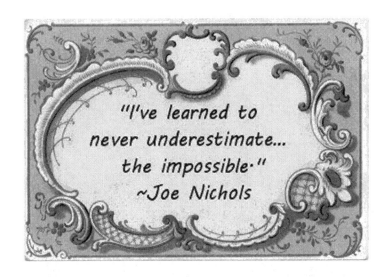

THE IMPOSSIBLE

A few years ago, I became involved with Addict II Athlete, an amazing organization, which gives recovering addicts an opportunity to become athletes. Their mantra is "Erase and Replace." They replace addictions and other things holding us back with running. And running. And running some more.

I got involved with this group because its founder is a good friend of mine, and I heard such wonderful things that were happening there. I was asked to speak to the group and tell my story. I must say the things that have happened (and are still happening) since that night I can only describe as miraculous.

It was love at first sight. I knew the second I walked in that room that this wasn't just a group. There was just something much more. By the end of my presentation, I was overwhelmed with the fact that most of the people there had known, seen, *and* hit rock bottom—the very depths of hell—and were fighting, becoming, and *are* some of the greatest, strongest people I have ever known. The only thing bigger than their strength was their hearts. In just a few months, I formed friendships with people who are dearer to my heart than I have in my whole life. I came to speak to a group, and what I found was a family.

In the weeks that came, I got to know more and more members of my new family through social media. I remember one of my now very good friends, Wade, wasn't at my presentation. Every time I'd post something hilarious (or so I thought) about "Running isn't possible for this wiggly chick!" Wade would reply (more like *preach*) that anything is possible and I needed to change my attitude. I'd just roll my eyes and think of how he didn't know I had cerebral palsy, and how he'd feel horrible once he met me. Oh how wrong I was.

When I finally met Wade, there was no hesitation from him...no, "Oh!" micro-expression people have when they see me for the first time. Just the biggest, most heartfelt hug I'd had in a long time. I'll never ever forget that hug. And as I got to know Wade more and more, I realized he spoke the truth. I *did* need to change my attitude. I just didn't know it yet.

As I continued to attend the of AIIA meetings, I noticed a theme forming around the things that were talked about. What they *didn't* talk about was addictions, cravings, sad stories. They *did* talk about doing hard things. And the hard things becoming amazing things. They talked about running; not just running, but becoming athletes and champions. They talked about service, and the importance of lifting each other up. But the thing I kept hearing more and more from these amazing athletes was "Never in a million years did I think I was capable of becoming an athlete!"

These words, and the wise words of Wade stayed with me, every day, every night. I had no idea how they would change my life.

Addict II Athlete was sponsoring a big event in Utah County called the Village Run. It was a 5k run open to the public, with all the proceeds going to Utah Foster Care Foundation. The spirit of giving caught hold of me. I wanted to be involved. My two boys were graciously given entries to the run, and we donated a drop in the bucket for the foster kids, but I wanted to do more. A member of the AIIA family had a motorized scooter he offered to me so I could "ride" alongside my boys.

It was a good plan. A great plan. My new family was making sure I was involved; that love shining through again.

But those words, "Never in a million years did I think I was capable of becoming an athlete!" seemed to be haunting me. I made a decision. I was going to do the 5k. Not in the motorized scooter, but on my own two feet. I kept it a secret for about a week. I guess I hadn't fully committed yet.

On a Friday, I walked a mile. The next Monday, I walked two miles in the afternoon, then another mile that evening. The 5k was Saturday. I had announced I would walk the 5k earlier that week, but later as I walked my last mile, I had serious doubts. I was tired, and I hurt so very much.

A couple nights before the 5k, Jeff, another AIIA champion, offered to run the course with me. Jeff, who has been through hell and back and now runs marathons right and left and teaches the rest of us how to do the same. Jeff, who while running his own race, noticed an inexperienced runner and slowed down to run with him. And when his new friend's shoes started to fall apart, Jeff took his own shoes off and gave them to the young runner so *he* could finish the race. Jeff, who stayed with him to the end, running barefoot the rest of the way. Jeff, the friend everyone wishes they had. Jeff, whose heart knows no limits.

That night, Jeff walked with my boys and me, at a snail's pace, encouraging me, laughing with me, giving my guys running tips. Every time I tried to apologize for being so slow, he'd tell me there was no place he'd rather be. And he meant it. As he dropped us off that night, the pain got to me and I became very emotional and started to doubt if I could do this. Jeff's response? Not a generic, "Aww, Jeni, just do your best." Nope, Jeff told it like it was. Like it was literally a matter of fact, he said, "Of course you can. You just did." And that was that. Those words would later provide more encouragement than I could ever express.

I woke up the day before the run…to snow. It had been spring weather for over a month, but like all springs here in Utah, there's always one last storm. This was it. And the promise of more snow for Saturday. Those who know me know there's nothing harder for me than to walk in snow and ice. Every muscle in my body tenses tighter and tighter. And if that weren't bad enough, I had a serious cold brewing. By Friday night, I was feverish and miserable, and was seriously considering backing out. Surely, I deserved better conditions for my first 5k, right?

Then suddenly, my mind and heart were flooded with words. The words of Wade, and Jeff, and Sarah, and Terri, and Jed, and Lana, and Keith, and Ginger, and Tyler, and Brandon, and Jarom, and everyone else in my AIIA family. The words of my heroes, Chad Hymas, Art Berg, Nick Vujicic.

"Doing what must be done."

"The impossible just takes a little longer."

"With God, miracles happen."

I was overwhelmed with courage and strength.

I awoke Saturday to two feet of snow, and it was still coming down. I was about to panic when I got a text from my Jeff:

"Jeni, you got this. One step at a time."

By the way, Jeff was on his way to do a 50k—thirty miles! And he took the time to encourage *me!* Wow. That was exactly what I needed to remind myself that yes, I *was* doing this.

We got there and started with style. My boys finished half the course, with their heads held high. I'm so proud of them. I had two angels from AIIA by my side the whole run. Lana and Ginger, now best friends for life, never left my side. They up-lifted me more than I can express, and I'll love them both forever.

Somewhere in the middle there, I was told, "Oh by the way, this is actually closer to a 6k, not a 5k." All righty then.

The course required us to loop around twice, so that halfway through, it would have been easy to give up, go inside, and get warm. Most of the two hundred runners had already finished their second lap anyway. I felt awful for taking up the time of all the amazing volunteers, especially the ones standing out in the snow with signs telling us which way to go. But I HAD to finish this. For my boys. For the foster teens. For my AIIA family. For me.

I was hurting. I didn't know what time it was. I didn't care. Every step took more concentra-tion—and caused more pain. I didn't want to chat with my girls anymore. At the end, I don't even think I could. Members of my team were trickling back to walk with me, to encourage me. My heart was overwhelmed by their patience and love. But I was beat, and starting to doubt again.

Then came Daniel. He had been my neighbor for five years and I had watched him grow into an amazing young man. He was one of the volunteers who stood in the snow, showing us where to go. He was at the LAST corner, so he was standing there the longest. And because of me, he and all of the other volunteers had to stand in the freezing cold a lot longer than they signed up for. I told him that we were the caboose and to go get warm. For a minute I think he did, but then he came jogging toward us. I looked at him and said, "I told you that you were done, kid…you've done so much already." I'll never forget this sweet boy's words. "I'm done when Jeni's done." Just when I thought I couldn't take another step, my Daniel gave me wings.

An hour and forty-six minutes after I started the Village Run, I crossed the finish line with my head held high, my posse of angels by my side, and my AIIA family applauding, high-fiving, and hugging me. I did it! But did what? I was still a bit blurry and numb.

Then came support from all my teammates with hugs and high fives. As I was trying to process the emotions, which were starting to flood in, Marissa—one of my best and dearest friends—grabbed me by the shoulders, practically shaking me, looked me square in the eyes, and said, "Do you know what you just *did*?"

I lost it. Bawled like a baby in her arms. The love, the support, the angels, the miracles of that day rushed through me all at once, and yes, I knew what I had done:

The Impossible.

VILLAGE RUN
March 23, 2013

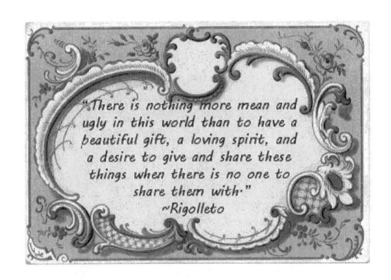

"There is nothing more mean and ugly in this world than to have a beautiful gift, a loving spirit, and a desire to give and share these things when there is no one to share them with."
~Rigolleto

DOLLAR STORE ANGEL

I love dollar stores. I'm like a kid in a, well, dollar store.

It's where I go to get rewards for my kids, *it's-the-thought-that-counts* gifts for my friends, and *just because* treats for myself.

Heaven knows I don't need a legitimate excuse to fall, but this time I had one. I was looking at the cute little baskets…making up a reason to buy a couple, and *BOOM!*

My foot found a misplaced box in the middle of the aisle, and I went down. *Hard.* Not only did I land flat on my face—spread eagle—but I managed to take down a six-foot-tall stack of display boxes at the end of the aisle.

I always try to notice the things that go through my mind immediately after a fall. As the dust settled, my thoughts were (in this order) …

119

Who saw me fall? (Anything under three people is a plus.)

Was I bleeding?

Please don't let those boxes be filled with little porcelain baby Jesuses! I pictured the shattered pieces all over the floor and knew I'd go straight to hell if this were the case.

Luckily, only one person saw, there was no signs of bleeding, and the boxes were filled with generic bags of potato chips. *Whew!*

But as they say, the story doesn't end there. The one person who saw me fall was a sweet middle-aged lady. She rushed over and helped me up. I realized right away there was a language barrier as she asked over and over, "You okay, yes?" I just smiled, very embarrassed, and kept thanking her.

When we finally completed the task of getting me back on my feet, she took my hand, wrapped it around a sturdy shelf, and said sternly, but with a smile, "You stay here!" She then turned around and proceeded to pick up the boxes and the potato chips that were scattered all over the aisle. After a few seconds, I bent over to help. Again, she took my hand, put it back on the shelf, and said, "No-no-no. You stay here."

Something in her face and tone told me I needed to do what I was told. I stood there helpless, watching this sweet woman clean up *my* mess. When she was finished, she turned around and once more asked, "You okay, yes?"

I was overwhelmed. I wanted to tell her how grateful I was. How she made my day so much better. What an amazing person she was. Instead, I hugged her and whispered in her ear, "You are beautiful," and hoped with all my heart that she understood. Then, we both went our ways and that was that.

Except it wasn't. The *don't-miss-it* thing kicked in.

As I replayed the whole fiasco in my head, it hit me. This wasn't *my* story, it was hers. It was about the beautiful stranger who took time out of her busy day to *literally* pick me up.

I started playing the *what-if* game.

What if she was having a terrible day and found some peace knowing she helped someone else?

What if in her morning prayers, she asked to be an instrument in God's hands and recognized this as an answer to her prayer?

What if...just what if...she was so downtrodden and frustrated for being seen as just another frustrating non-English speaker in an English-speaking world. What if that day she really needed someone to see her *heart.*

That I did, and it was as big as the whole world.

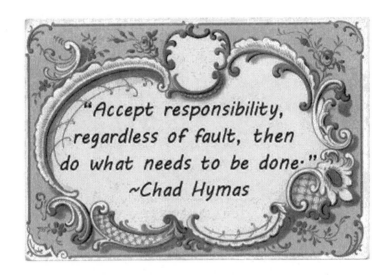

"Accept responsibility, regardless of fault, then do what needs to be done."
~Chad Hymas

THE INCIDENTAL IMPROV

While discovering that I did in fact, have a story to tell, I was encouraged to reach out to a guy named Chad Hymas. If you don't know who he is, Google him. Seriously, right now. I could *never* do this man justice. Let's try anyway, shall we?

Chad owns an elk farm in northern Utah. One day, a one ton-bale of hay fell on him—paralyzing him from the armpits down. Chad went on to do the impossible, and now travels around the world telling *his* story.

I won't lie. When I started finding out about him, I thought, "Great. *Another* guy with a life-changing, really, *really* tough experience who overcomes all, and is worshipped by millions." And as I've thought a million times before, he is *NOTHING like me.*

I did some research and was shocked into an amazing respect for this man. He truly became a hero as I learned more of his story. My doubts that we didn't have anything in common melted away as I realized part of this great man's story included times of bitterness and anger. AND he still inspired.

An amazing opportunity presented itself when our church youth program hosted an event in the beautiful mountains of Aspen Grove, Utah. The leaders—who included some close friends of mine—asked Chad to speak at the conference…and he said yes!

I was invited to go hear him speak *and* possibly meet him. Giddy with excitement, I set off with the group into the snow-filled mountains. Our little caravan arrived early, and I got a great seat up front. As I scanned the room, I became overwhelmed as it filled to capacity with excited teenagers.

About ten minutes before Chad was to take the stage, I noticed that my leader friends were texting frantically as they paced faster and faster in front of me. Looking around, I noticed that Chad hadn't arrived yet, and the clock was ticking. Five minutes later, I made eye contact with my buddy, Blu, and I knew in my heart what was going to happen next. He came over, sat down by me, took my hand, and said, "Jeni, we need you." Those words became a pivotal bookmark in my story. I nodded with some apprehension, and that was that.

The meeting started, and Blu announced that I would be filling in until Chad arrived. The floodgates to my armpits opened as I realized I had nothing, *nothing* prepared. My mind went blank. What was my name again? But just as fast as my panic surfaced, it halted to a stop when I heard the quiet, yet piercing voice in my head reiterate, "You are *needed*," and perhaps more penetrating, "Yes, you *are* prepared."

With newfound confidence, I wiggled up to the podium and turned around. That's when the *first* of many miracles of the night happened. As I peered at my audience—two hundred youth and their leaders—a warm, overwhelming chill moved through me. These kids, these beautiful teenagers…*shined*. That's the only descriptive word that makes sense in my head. Their glow inspired the heck out of me, and I realized I was in the presence of the most elite, stalwart people on earth. That picture will forever be etched into my memory.

I don't remember what I said. Only that I opened my mouth and had faith that God would do the rest. He did. I spoke for twenty minutes until Chad rolled in and thankfully took over.

I now jokingly say that I once opened for a rock star! Second miracle of the night—check.

Chad took the stage and it was everything I expected...and more. His story touched and inspired me like no other (seriously, guys, put down this book and go order his). When he finished, the powerful feelings that he brought with him lingered through the whole room. As the meeting came to an end, the third miracle of the night took place. This will forever be one of my most wonderful, life-changing experiences.

I didn't see her coming. Before I could even stand up, she was there in front of me, embracing me with both arms and quietly crying on my shoulder. Though confused, I held her tightly. When she pulled away, wiping her tears, she said, "Jeni, I need to let you know that the reason Chad was late tonight was because of me." Still confused, I waited for her to continue. "I have been struggling with some really tough challenges. I've asked my leaders and parents for advice. I pray often, but haven't found peace. But tonight, Jeni, tonight God answered my prayers through you. The things you said, it's like you...*knew* somehow, exactly what I needed to hear."

I was speechless as she hugged me again. The only thing that I could think to tell her was how very beautiful she was. Lame I know, but I meant it with everything in my heart. She hugged me again, thanked me, and walked away. It was then I noticed the line of people behind her. All waiting to hug me and thank me for my words. All with similar stories of struggles and trials, which comes with being the amazing teens they are. They were *all* so very beautiful. I felt their strong Spirits and big hearts as I hugged them.

As I hugged the last kid, I felt overwhelmed, stunned, and numb at the same time. My brain was trying to make sense of what my heart had just experienced. I thought it would take a while to process, but surprisingly, what I needed to know hit me as I was riding the elevator at the end of the night.

That night, that experience, wasn't about me. It *wasn't* about me. Chad being late, the wonderful experience of being able to fill in for him, the self-confidence it gave me, the love I felt and the beautiful connection with the youth I enjoyed afterward, nope. None of that was about me. Heck, it wasn't even about Chad Hymas, as amazing as he is. That night, that meeting, the twists and turns and how things played out, was about the sweet, beautiful, fourteen-year-old who was put in my path so that she could feel loved and *know* that she mattered.

This realization absolutely blew me away.

When I share my story, it's *never* about me. Ever. It's about you, my audience; my readers. Every time I choose to share my story, it's because someone, somewhere, needs to hear it. It sounds so boastful, and believe me, I doubt this more than I should, but when I have something that can help someone else, isn't it my duty to give that to others? I'm not a natural speaker. I don't have that natural flair and presence of a motivational speaker who engages audiences. I speak slowly and am kind of hard to understand. Yet for some odd reason, my stories, imperfections and all, inspire and entertain. So, I share them, allowing you to feel what you're going to feel. And so I don't forget about that beautiful girl whose prayers were answered because a world-renowned speaker was late.

It was never about me.

"My hand trembles, but my heart does not." ~Stephen Hopkins

KEVIN'S STORY

A hundred years ago when I was single the *first* time, I was a youth counselor. Best three summers of my life. I got to travel, teach, and have sleepovers with up to eighteen giggly teenage gals every night. Who wouldn't love it?

I admit I was a bit anxious when I started this venture, because I was working with the best of the best. Only about twenty-five percent of applicants were chosen for interviews, and from that twenty-five percent, only another twenty-five percent were hired. The other counselors were so confident, so happy, and well, very able-bodied. It was a bit intimidating. I worried that when I introduced myself to my girls, they would think, "Man! Why'd I get the broken counselor?" But, by the end of the day, I found a way to put their minds at ease, and we always had a heck of a week.

Along with being in charge of my own little group of gals, I got to team up with a fellow counselor and his group of guys. (Flirting was encouraged among the youth...not among the counselors. Although—never mind—a story for another time.) I loved my guys as much as I loved my gals. I could see potential husbands and fathers in them, and was overwhelmed at their greatness. And somehow having me as one of their counselors brought out the gentleness and protectiveness in them. By the end of each week, I had sixteen guys who treated me like a queen (not to mention my own eager personal assistants; I almost never had to carry my own backpack...it was so very sweet). It was easy to then remind them that I had sixteen girls who in turn, needed to be treated like princesses. And they always did.

Kevin was one of my guys. He was sixteen and amazing. I'll never forget his smile and his big heart. Right away I noticed he hung out beside me ALL the time. At first I thought he had a little crush on me, but deep in my heart I knew this was something else. Something more important. Wherever we went as a group (there was always around forty of us as a group), he was always close by, watching. If I dropped so much as a pencil, Kevin was there, emerging from our group to quickly pick it up for me.

There were a couple of dances every week at EFY. Our job as counselors was to make sure these teens were having fun, but not too *much* fun. My Kevin always wanted to dance with me. I kept trying to point out all the cute girls he should ask to dance, but he kept coming back and asking me to dance...especially the slow dances. Again, something told me he needed this.

At the end of each week, we would get together in groups of a hundred to let the youth stand and share their experiences and feelings about the week. It was always my favorite part of the week, because I could see the absolute greatness in these kids. It was always a very spiritual experience.

When my Kevin stood up, he shared some amazing insights of the week, and I felt so proud of this young man. He then turned to me and looked me in the eyes. As his voice cracked and with tears running down his face, he said, "Thank you, Jeni." As he paused to collect his thoughts and wipe his tears, I was a little shocked. It was *he* who had helped *me* all week. What he said next would change my life forever.

"I have a sister who is disabled. She died last year. She never walked and could barely talk. I always wanted to know how to help her; how to *hear* her. When she died, I didn't know if she even knew how much I loved her."

He paused to wipe his eyes then looked at me again.

"When I met you on Monday, I felt the same spirit of love imitating out of you that I felt from her. And I wanted to be around you. I miss her so much. And somehow, I felt when I was helping you, I was helping her. At the dances, I imagined her dancing on her own legs, and laughing and joking as brothers and sisters do. So thank you, Jeni, for letting me hang out with you this week; for letting me serve you, letting me carry your stuff, and yes, for dancing with me. I finally feel like I have closure; and that yes, my sister does know how much I love her."

Wow. As I sat there, wiping my own eyes, I realized something that was so important that even now, twenty years later, I'm blown away. Most of my life I had been trying to prove myself. To show the world that I could be amazing despite my wiggly body. That my disability was something to overcome; to shove to the back corner of my life.

That Saturday night, I realized I had given my Kevin something that no other counselor could give him, not DESPITE my disability, but BECAUSE of it. Because we were all designed to be perfectly imperfect, I was able to help this amazing young man find the peace that he had been looking for so long. Again, wow.

It was never about me.

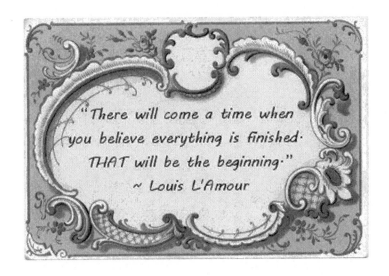

"There will come a time when you believe everything is finished. THAT will be the beginning."
~ Louis L'Amour

HERE WE GO AGAIN...

Just recently I was at my neurologist—a cerebral palsy specialist. I told him I had a new goal. He asked what it was, and I grinned and said, "Doc, I wanna RUN!" He paused to see if I was kidding. Then he said,

"Jeni, you realize that this may never be possible, right?" I'm sure that I confused the heck out of him when I cocked my head, put on my best ornery smile and said,

"Did you just tell me that running is…*impossible*?"

Watch this.

***

Oh yeah, one more thing. A few years ago, a friend introduced me to a quotation by author Marianne Williamson. It changed my life, and is what gave me the courage to finally finish this book (and I use "finish" very lightly, because there are tons more stories waiting to be written). Take a read:

> "Our deepest fear is not that we are inadequate. Our deepest fear is that we are powerful beyond measure. It is our light, not our darkness that most frightens us. We ask ourselves, 'Who am I to be brilliant, gorgeous, talented, fabulous?'
>
> Actually, who are you *not* to be? You are a child of God. Your playing small does not serve the world. There is nothing enlightened about shrinking so that other people won't feel insecure around you. We are all meant to shine, as children do. We were born to make manifest the glory of God that is within us. It's not just in some of us; it's in everyone. And as we let our own light shine, we unconsciously give other people permission to do the same. As we are liberated from our own fear, our presence automatically liberates others."
>
> ~Marianne Williamson

As a personal favor to me, could ya just go back and read that again? I'll wait…(It took me reading it about fifteen times to finally *start* to sink in.)

See, being afraid of failure is easy. It's not fun, but it's easy. But for some reason the thought of shining light upon ourselves for the whole world to see—imperfections and all—and to realize that our imperfections allow us to change lives—Holy cow that's scary! And it's also very, very true.

At the beginning of my book, I told you I hoped that in reading *my* story, you would find yours. I'd like to make that challenge official. Think about that perfectly imperfect part of yourself, the one that makes you cringe when you think about it, and not only give yourself a break, but realize that this imperfection of yours is a perfect inspiration for those around you. Realize it, and then own it.

"Your playing small does not serve the world."

Tell your story. Whether in a journal, or on a stage in front of a thousand people. Your perfect imperfections do and will inspire others.

Wiggle on, my friends, wiggle on!

BIBLIOGRAPHY

Goldman's Cecil Medicine. 24th ed. Philadelphia, PA: Elsevier Saunders; 2011

Tierney, John. "David Blaine Sets Breath-Holding Record". The New York Times. 4-30-2008

Williams, Marianne. A Return to Love: Reflections on the Principles of a Course in Miracles. HarperOne; Reissue edition. 1996

Contact, Watch, Listen and Laugh:

www.JeniRoper.com

Made in the USA
San Bernardino, CA
03 February 2020